# Shorty's Prayer

BY

# THABILE GLORIA MTSHALI

Published in 2022
Burning Books Publishing
www.amazon.com/author/burning

## Shorty's prayer

Baba wethu osezulwini,

malingcweliswe igama lakho;

mawufike umbuso wakho;

mayenziwe intando yakho

emhlabeni njengasezulwini;

usiphe namuhla isinkwa sethu semihla

ngemihla;

usithethelele amacala ethu,

njengalokhu nathi sibathethelela abasonayo;

ungasingenisi ekulingweni,

kodwa usikhulule kokubi;

ngokuba umbuso ungowakho,

namandla, nenkazimulo, kuze kubephakade.

Nge gama lika Jesus Christ.

Amen.

## Tears of a child

Tears of a child
Tears of a child
Tears of a child are being heard from a distance
A distance
A distant screaming and shouting for help
While a stranger is taking advantage of that
little child
Who is young and confused

Tears of a child
Tears of a child
Tears of a child are being seen by a stranger
walking far
Far
Far away
Screaming and crying for help
While the mother is drinking and drinking
Alcohol in the street
Forgetting about the innocent child
Who is young and confused

Tears of a child
Tears of a child
Tears of a child are being pushed away with
anger
To the other side of the corner
Nobody cares
No one cares for the little child who knows
nothing
Nothing at all

♠

Tears of a child
Tears of a child
Tears of a child are being hated and judged
Blamed by stupid people who don't have love at
all
For the little child who knows nothing
Nothing at all

♠

My loving God look at this
It breaks my poor little heart
Every day I walk around the township
I see
I hear
Those loud sad heartbreaking
Tears of a child

**Thoughts**

I am what I think I am.

What I am arises with my thoughts

That make the world go round.

Because my sole responsibility

Is the core quality

Of my full best mature fun good

Function of myself

Actualizing God the Creator

In every poem I write & recite

My party people.

## I am hunger

I reach among the people like a gloom
I reach down by each man's edge
But look
None of them recognize me
They look on one another and know I am there

My stillness is like the stillness of the tide
That buries the playground of the children
Like the profound frost in the slow night
When the birds are lifeless in the morning

Armies march, attack, raze & ruin with guns
Roaring from earth to air
I am more frightful than the armies
I am more frightening than the cannon

Kings and chancellors give commands
But look at me
I give no command to anyone
But everyone listens to me more than kings
And more than the passionate orators

I am the super one
I unswear words and undo deeds
Naked things know I am the first and the last
To be felt of the living
I am hunger

**Thoughts**

Shout out to myself

Because I am soooooo lit.

I mean like bheka.

I am very very lit, baba.

## Tears of a man

Tears of a man
Tears of a man
Tears of a man are being heard from a distance
A distance
A distant screaming and shouting for help
In the middle of sadness
Hear oh Lord, have mercy on me
I'm a paternal who's unemployed
And have nothing, nothing to
Support and feed my household everyday

Tears of a man
Tears of a man
Tears of a man are being heard and seen by a
strange woman walking far
Far
Far away
Screaming and shouting for help
In the middle of sadness
Hear oh Lord, have mercy on me
I'm a paternal
A paternal
A man who has nothing, nothing at all
To put on the table for my household
Every now and then

Tears of a man
Tears of a man
Tears of a man are being hated and pushed
away with anger
Hear oh Lord, have mercy on me
I'm a paternal who's an alcoholic
I have no work
Everywhere I go people laugh
And turn me into a joke

♠

Tears of a man
Tears of a man
Tears of a man are being blamed and judged
While screeching and yelling for help
In the middle of sadness and pain
Hear oh Lord, have mercy on me
I'm a paternal who's been beaten
By a wife everyday
People laugh at me because I have no power
No power at all

♠

Tears of a man
Tears of a man
Tears of a man are being laughed at
And turned into a comedy
When he weeps
Eeeiiissshhh
When a poor paternal weeps and weeps
In the middle of sadness and pain
Hear oh Lord, have mercy on me
I'm a paternal, a man who has nothing
Nothing at all for my household
My family is being pointed at and called evil
names
Each and every day
Because I'm a paternal, a man who is
powerless
Powerless
Powerless
Eeeiiissshhh
♠

My dear God please help
Hear that poor paternal
Hear that poor man
Hear that poor father
Who screeches and yells
Every day I walk around the township
I hear, I see, those loud sad heartbreaking
Tears of a man

## Thoughts

My life is just a wonderful blessing from God.

Even darkness & silence, I always overcome

And learn from whatever state I may be in.

From whatever state I may face in life.

They keep me so wise & brave,

Making me strong & content

In my super-duper life.

My mission in life is not merely to survive

But to strive to do my best with all

My good passion.

That's right, with all my super compassion.

With all my humour and style.

In every poem & every word.

## They call me Peter Stuyvesant

They call me Peter Stuyvesant
Because I am a heavy smoker
I was sent by John Rolfe
To say that Miss Courtleigh is dead

♠

When I crossed the filter I met
Two guys Benson & Hedges
Who tried to rob my Gold Leaf
So I took out my Gunston and shot
Between Lexington and Camel

♠

Mr Albany took me to jail
In jail I took out my Consulate
And I consoled myself

♠

B&B was the judge and
Craven A was my stupid lawyer
Who fought to save me
And Remington Gold
When Marlboro Beyond Blue was angry
Wanting to kill Chesterfield because
The Kingston and Savannah
Had an argument in Virginia
Yeah, they call me Peter Stuyvesant

## Thoughts

My most essential ingredient

That's so effective in my poetry,

In my art and communication.

It helps me to build my big foundation

And principles that help me keep

My relationships and friendships

Growing strong and wise every day.

Prayer.

## That girl

It's December time
Everybody is out and about
On vacations
The lanes are tranquil
She's alone, desolated and lonely
She has nowhere to go
That female

I'm talking about that female
That female that's been taken
For granted each and every day
Walking up and down the lane
With a torn heart
That miss

I'm talking about that miss
That miss that's been called
By evil names every now and then
That lass

♠

I'm talking about that lass
That lass that's been judged
During winter time
Cold and shaking
Shivering and crying
That damsel

♠

I'm talking about that damsel
That damsel that's been
Turned into a black sheep
Blamed for everything
After her mom died
That maiden

♠

I'm talking about that poor maiden
That maiden that's been raped
Several times
Not finding help
She feels like a stranger
That girl

♠

I'm talking about that girl
That girl that's been abused
And hurt most of her life
It's December time
Everybody is out and about
On vacations
The lanes are tranquil
She's lonely and desolated
She has nowhere to go
That girl

## Thoughts

I believe in myself.

I have faith in all my abilities.

Because my humble heart has many reasons

And positive powers that keep me strong,

Always and every day,

So I can be happy though dark days

And be wiser and more successful

In my super-duper crazy loving life.

**That day, that month, that year**

25 February 2022
Is the day, the month, the year
I will never forget
I was born and raised in a township
With a dream of being a healer
While my family hoped and wished
That I should study and be rich
For the rest of my life
♠

They wished and hoped that I
Should study and be the best
Doctor, nurse, teacher, lawyer
Pilot, policewoman, and working
At the bank earning good cash
They motivated me to study
So I could be rich and wealthy
But
♠

That's not me
That's not my dream
I don't wanna be a
Doctor, nurse, teacher, lawyer
I never dreamed of working at the bank
My dream is to see myself
Healing and entertaining people
People
People who are torn apart
People with broken hearts
♠

The same people who should support me
The same people who should encourage me
Took me for granted and never believed in me
Because they wanted me to be
What they hoped and wished for
♠
While deep in myself
Deep, deep, deep inside my soul
I see healing… entertainment
And motivation
♠
I see myself entertaining
Healing
And motivating people with broken hearts
♠
My family stopped believing in me
Because they saw blessings, lights
And more down inside me
They called me by names
Splintering evil words that made
Them think I would give up on myself
Fissuring bad words that made them think
I would give up on my dreams and goals
But
♠

Look at me
I never give up on my dreams and goals
Look at me right now
I will never give up on myself
Because
God gave me power to heal
God gave me blessings to restore
And entertain every broken heart

♠

They turned me down with one hope
Of seeing me hopeless and fruitless
Because they see more boon that's
Inside my skull
They see more intelligent gifts inside my spirit
They vagrant my existence
Pulling me down so that
I may stop believing in myself
But

♠

Look at me
I'm out and about in the darkness
I'm secluded with no one to comfort me
But still I never forgot what God gave me
To inhabit this beautiful world
But still I never forgot that
I am a warrior woman
I am a soldier woman
I see the future in the fixture
I am my brother's sister
My father's keeper

♠

Still no one can pull and drag me down
Even though I'm homeless
Look at me
I'm never homeless
Because God keeps telling me
I am a star

♠

I am a star when
That day, that month, that year
I will never forget
While so many haters took me for granted
Not knowing that I am loved and known
By Jesus Christ who made me heard
On that day, that month, that year
When I found myself in the middle of the stage
Screaming and shouting
People I am loved by God
Who made me a star
A warrior woman
A soldier woman
Who sees the future in the fixture
I am my brother's sister
My father's keeper

♠

25 February 2022
Is the day, the month, the year
I will never forget in my super-duper life
When I turned the haters down
Look at me right now
I am listened to more than the passionate
haters
I am standing in the middle of the stage
Motivating and healing broken hearts
♠

25 February 2022
Is the day, the month, the year
I will never forget

## Thoughts

Happiness is not about getting what I want.

It's about everything I have

In my super-duper life

That God the creator gave me

To inhabit this beautiful world.

## No more tears

No more tears
To fall from my eyes
No more tears
To exhibit with that broken footstep to echo
Just that frenzy poem to motivate
My poor soul every day

♠

No more tears
No more wishing I could die
Because I hated life
No more doubting my dreams and goals
Because I was blinded by the explosion
Of being called a loser
Who's not gonna make it

♠

No more tears
No more apologies to record
For being blamed for things I've never done
Because I'm hated
No more wishing I could buy and sell
Things that could make me rich and worthy
For the rest of my poor sad life
But

♠

But only this precious and special gift
A talent God gave me
To inhabit this beautiful world

♠

No more tears
Firstly I used to long for love
Over and over
Firstly I used to think my passion was finished
Because of the first shot I heard fired
Fired by the brightness chasing away the
darkness
The darkness
The darkness that became the past

♠

Look at me these days
All those nervous nights and broken mornings
Are gone
Gone forever

♠

Look at me these days
All those nervous nights and broken mornings
All those blinded evenings
Are gone
Gone forever
In the singing of the song
In my body and your body
The knowledge still remains that
The final battle is
I've conquered the darkness
I've made it
No more tears

# Thoughts

My strong positive attitude creates more mental miracles than any drug.

I don't change my attitude based on what people say, because at the end of the day they're just judging me from their own perspective.

They don't know me.

I'll just be myself, and let people love and accept me for who I am, not someone I'm not.

**Life! What is life?**

Life
What is life
I seem to be confused
Sitting on my own thinking to myself

♠

Life is hard sometimes
My existence is puzzling sometimes
Life is great sometimes
My being is vast sometimes
Life is bad sometimes
My energy is spoiled sometimes
Life is good sometimes
My spirit is admirable sometimes

♠

But still I'm blind and confused
Sitting on my own in the middle of life
Asking myself questions questions questions

♠

Life
What is life
I seem to be confused
Sitting on my own in the corner
Darkness blinded by the
Explosion of
Life is hard sometimes
Life is great sometimes
Life is bad sometimes
Life is good sometimes

♠

I'm alone in the middle of life
Asking myself questions
Every now and then because
My existence is hard
My being is great
My energy is bad
My spirit is good sometimes
♠

When I'm about to give up
On myself and life
So blind and confused
Lost in the middle of life
Not knowing that my life
Is a blessing from God
My life is a lesson from God
That I should learn and study to be
Wise brave and strong
♠

When I make it through hard and sore
When I make it through good and great
While some around me commit suicide
Not able to face life on its own
Not able to face life on its own terms
Zooming around and round
So lost and confused
Asking myself questions
Asking one another questions
Questions
♠

Life - What is life
I seem to be lost and confused

Sitting on my own in the middle of life
Thinking to myself
Why is my existence puzzling
Sometimes
Why is my being so vast
Sometimes
Why is my energy spoiled sometimes
Why is my spirit admirable
Sometimes

When I never knew that life is
What I build for myself
Life is what I make for myself
Through hard and great
Through bad and good
When I never knew that life is a
Beautiful gift from God
Happy are you when you've got life
So please my dear friend remember
Handle with care

Always remember that life
Is a lesson to be learned and studied
By all who have dreams and goals
Because I life ifana na ma dice
Sometimes U happy
Sometimes U ia khala
Forgetting that the knowledge always remains
That the final battle is
Life is good all the time
Life is great all the time

## Thoughts

Everywhere I go, people wonder

What makes me so strong, brave and wise.

It's because my best preparation for tomorrow

Is writing my best poems for today.

Because my yesterday was just a destiny

That keeps my every day with cool opportunity

To taste from the sweet wine of life.

## Farewell to my sadness and pain

Take it or leave it
These sad discussions have gone out
Each of these sad days and years has its value
When tears used to fall like
Money jangling in a cash register
Oh my word

I wish I could buy that good life
When out on the streets the sun is cruel
A CD player turns up
It's young money cash money billionaires
Playing for the rest of my life
Oh my

Am I gonna make it
When I sat alone with my quill
And my journal ready to give up
On myself and life
I wish I could die
Boom

That's when my lightning strikes
My journal and quill disgorge
A lamp of ideas
I turn the page and write myself a poem
Farewell to my sadness and pain
Yeah

That's right because it's either
You believe it or not
Take it or leave it nobody cares
Because a writer that knows the rules
The lightning strikes and misses
Sadness and pain come and go
Because I've already dropped everything
Now this is my final final final
Final
Farewell to my sadness and pain

## Thoughts

I am clothed with strength and dignity

That make me laugh without fearing the future.

**About the poet**

Shorty was raised by a single mother in Alexandra. From an early age, she wanted to be an entertainer. She loved singing and dancing. But when Shorty was 11, her mother passed away, and Shorty's dreams died too.

Years of abuse made her hate life. She lost focus. At 16, she had a son, now being raised by her sister. At 17, Shorty moved to Melville. Angry. Wanting to die.

But she found love on the streets of Johannesburg.

From 2007 she adapted to street life. She learned she had to depend on herself. She used to beg for money, until in 2016 – standing outside Poppy's – she showed her poems to a friend who suggested she should read them for people.

Today she is well-known on the streets of Melville, reciting her poetry to anyone who will take the time to listen to the heartfelt words of a true poet.

Check out her first book – Shorty's Poems.

You can find her online at

www.amazon.com/author/shorty or www.books2read.com/b/shorty

Watch "The Melville Poet" videos on YouTube. Shorty Malorty is a star, baby...

♠

Published 2022 by Burning Books Publishing

www.amazon.com/author/burning

If you'd like to contact Shorty, you can reach her through us, at BurningBooksPublishing@gmail.com. We'll pass on any messages or comments.